First Facts

GREAT LEADERS and THINKERS

of ~Ancient Greece~

by Megan Cooley Peterson

Consultant:
Jonathan M. Hall
Phyllis Fay Horton Distinguished Service Professor
in the Humanities
The University of Chicago

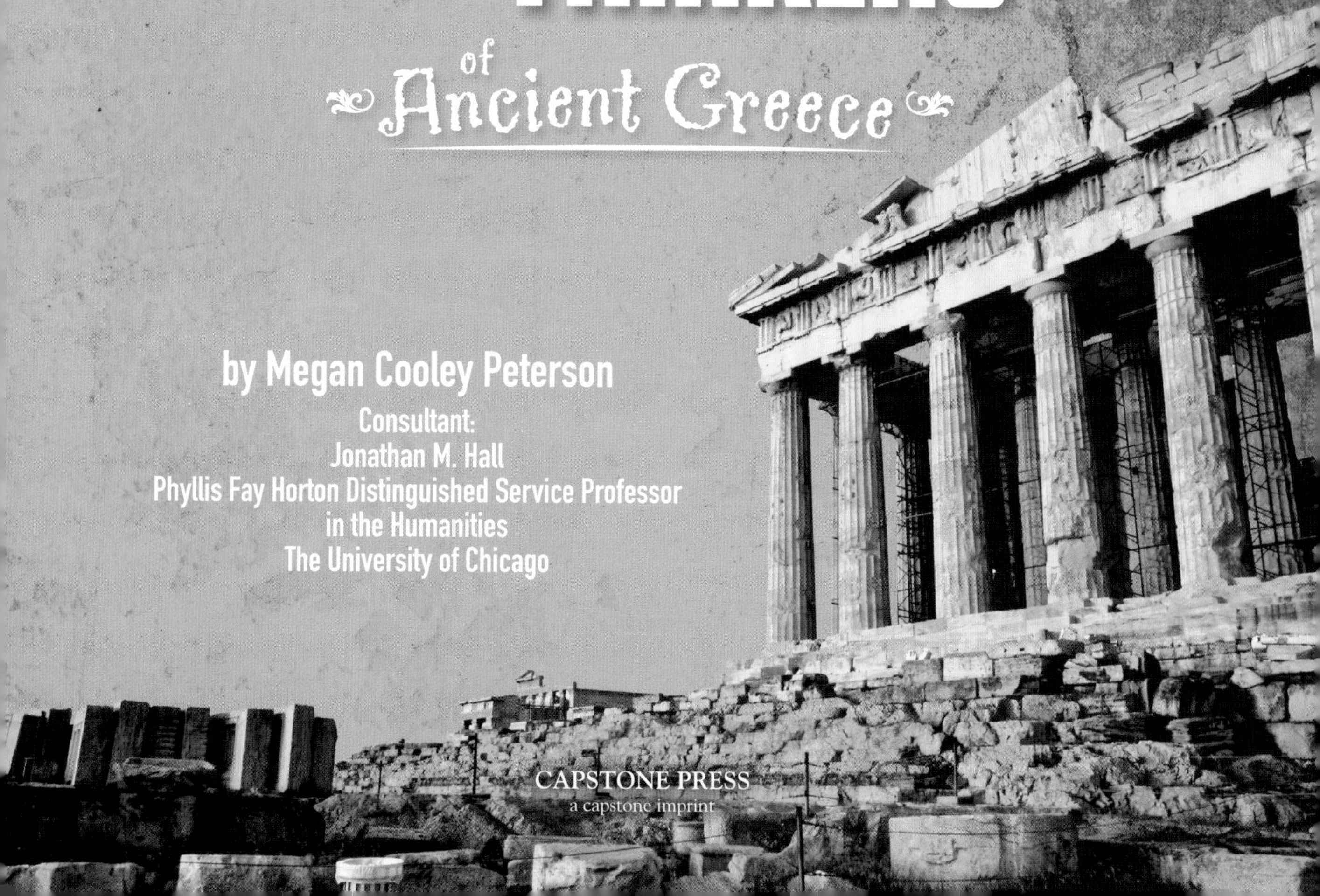

CAPSTONE PRESS
a capstone imprint

First Facts are published by Capstone Press,
1710 Roe Crest Drive, North Mankato, Minnesota 56003
www.capstonepub.com

Library of Congress Cataloging-in-Publication Data
Peterson, Megan Cooley.
Great leaders and thinkers of ancient Greece / Megan Cooley Peterson.
pages cm.—(Ancient Greece)
Includes bibliographical references and index.
ISBN 978-1-4914-0275-7 (library binding)
ISBN 978-1-4914-0280-1 (eBook PDF)
Summary: "Describes famous writers, philosophers, teachers, and political leaders of ancient Greece."—Provided by publisher.
1. Greece—Civilization—To 146 B.C.—Juvenile literature. 2. Civilization, Modern—Greek influences—Juvenile literature. I. Title.
DF77.P46 2015
938—dc23   2013049477

Editorial Credits

Aaron Sautter, editor; Bobbie Nuytten, designer; Svetlana Zhurkin, media researcher; Jennifer Walker, production specialist

Photo Credits

Getty Images: Kean Collection, 13, UIG, 8; iStockphotos: HultonArchive, 20; Newscom: akg-images, 7, 17, akg-images/Peter Connolly, 9, 19, Image Broker/BAO, 15; Shutterstock: Ensuper (paper), back cover and throughout, Georgy Markov, 6, ilolab (grunge background), cover, 1, Kamira, back cover (bottom right), 21, Lefteris Papaulakis, 11, marcokenya, cover (right), 1, Maxim Kostenko (background), 2 and throughout, mexrix, 5 (back), Nick Pavlakis, cover (left), 14, 16, Renata Sedmakova, 12, Roberto Castillo (column), back cover and throughout, Vladislav Gurfinkel, 10; SuperStock, 18; XNR Productions, 5 (map)

Printed in China by Nordica
0414/CA21400593
032014   008095NORDF14

TABLE OF CONTENTS

MAKING THE MODERN WORLD

Think about the last movie you saw at the theater. Can you imagine our world without movies or plays? What would life be like if people couldn't go to college or vote in elections? We can enjoy these things today thanks to ancient Greek leaders and thinkers. These people created the beginnings of modern science, **philosophy**, and **democracy**. Meet some of the ancient Greeks who helped shape our world.

philosophy—the study of truth and knowledge
democracy—a kind of government in which the people make decisions by voting

Ancient Greece, around 400 BC

• city-state (a city that is independent and is not part of a country)

Macedonia

Illyria

Epirus

Mt. Olympus ▲

Thessaly

Aegean Sea

Lesbos

Euboea

Delphi •

• Thebes

Attica

Corinth •

• Athens

Olympia •

• Argos

Peloponnesus

• Sparta

Rhodes

N
W · E
S

0   90 miles

0   90 kilometers

Crete

Mediterranean Sea

HOMER

(lived between 1200 BC and 750 BC)

The ancient Greeks enjoyed telling stories. The poet Homer created the famous poems the *Iliad* and the *Odyssey*. These **epic** poems describe a war between Greece and nearby Troy. No one knows if the Trojan War really happened. It might be a **myth**.

Homer's poems feature many Greek gods and goddesses. The Greeks often studied his poems to learn more about their gods.

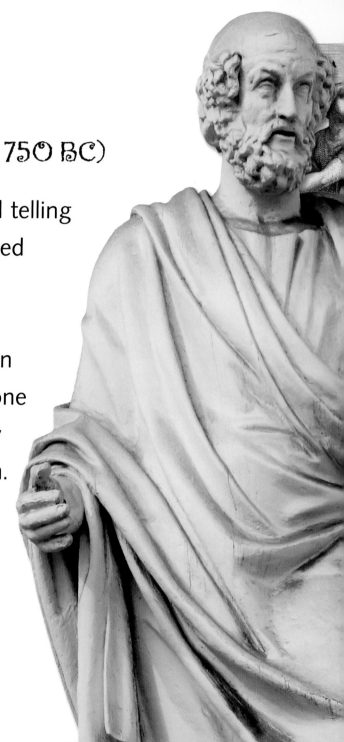

Homer's epic poems were often performed for an audience.

epic—relating to a long story about heroic adventures and great battles

myth—a story told by people in ancient times

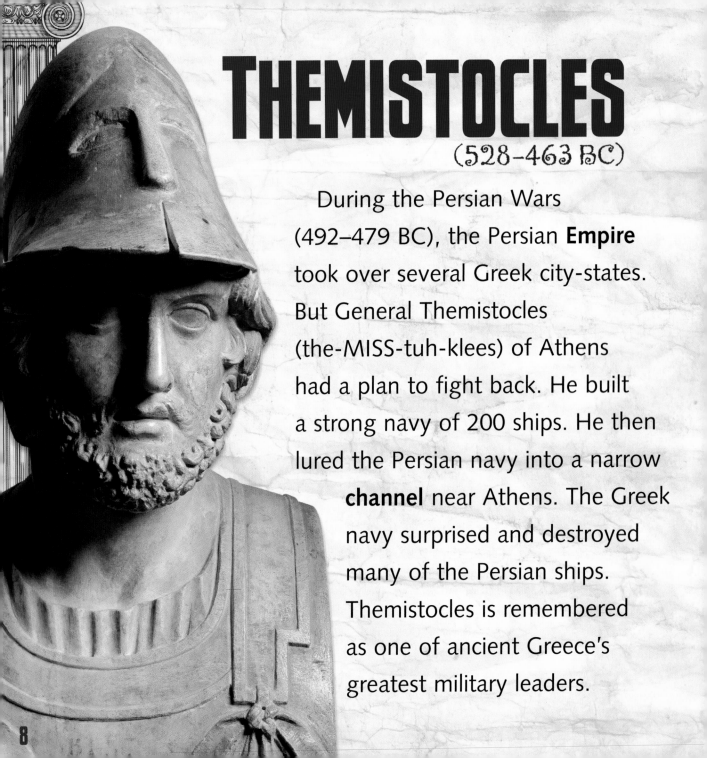

THEMISTOCLES

(528–463 BC)

During the Persian Wars (492–479 BC), the Persian **Empire** took over several Greek city-states. But General Themistocles (the-MISS-tuh-klees) of Athens had a plan to fight back. He built a strong navy of 200 ships. He then lured the Persian navy into a narrow **channel** near Athens. The Greek navy surprised and destroyed many of the Persian ships. Themistocles is remembered as one of ancient Greece's greatest military leaders.

empire—a large territory ruled by a powerful leader

channel—a narrow stretch of water between two areas of land

PERICLES (495–429 BC)

Pericles (PARE-uh-klees) is often called the greatest leader of ancient Athens. The people elected him at least 20 times. Pericles helped shape democracy in Athens during his 30-year rule. Pericles' greatest success was leading the building of the Acropolis. This group of **temples** sits on a hill overlooking Athens. Though damaged, the buildings still stand today.

FACT:

Pericles passed laws to help poor people. One law allowed the poor to see plays in theaters for free. Another law made sure that people were paid for working on a jury.

the Acropolis of Athens

temple—a building used for worship

HERODOTUS
(485–420 BC)

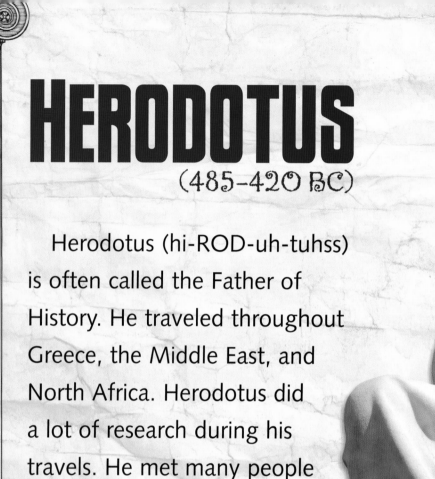

Herodotus (hi-ROD-uh-tuhss) is often called the Father of History. He traveled throughout Greece, the Middle East, and North Africa. Herodotus did a lot of research during his travels. He met many people and learned about their culture and history. He made sure he knew historical facts before writing about what he learned.

FACT:

Herodotus wrote a history of the Persian Wars called *The Histories*. Much of what we know about the Persian Wars comes from his writings.

Herodotus reads *The Histories* to a crowd of people.

PHIDIAS (490–425 BC)

Greek **sculptor** Phidias created one of the Seven Wonders of the Ancient World. He built a statue of the god Zeus seated on a throne. Made of ivory and gold, the statue was 45 feet (14 meters) tall. Phidias also designed and oversaw the building of the Parthenon. This temple for the goddess Athena was part of the Acropolis in Athens. It still stands today as one of the world's most famous buildings.

sculptor—a person who creates art by carving stone, wood, or other materials

the Parthenon

FACT:

The Lincoln Memorial in Washington, D.C., holds a statue of President Abraham Lincoln. It was modeled on Phidias' statue of Zeus.

Phidias' statue of Zeus, king of the gods

PLATO (427-347 BC)

Plato was one of history's greatest philosophers. He had new ideas for how nations should be run. Plato wrote about these ideas in *The Republic*.

He thought the country should be divided into three groups of people. Philosophers would run government. Warriors would keep people safe. And producers would grow food and build things people needed.

Plato taught at the Academy for 40 years.

PLATO'S GREATEST STUDENT

Plato also taught at the Academy, which he started in 387 BC. It was one of history's first schools of higher learning. The great Greek scientist, Aristotle, studied under Plato at the Academy for nearly 20 years. Aristotle was one of the first scientists to study plants, animals, and **physics**. His teachings guided scientists' thinking for about 2,000 years.

physics—science that studies matter, energy, force, and motion

ALEXANDER THE GREAT

(356-323 BC)

Alexander the Great was king of Macedonia, which controlled Greece at that time. He led his powerful army into many battles. Alexander created the largest empire the world had ever seen. It stretched nearly 3,000 miles (4,800 kilometers) from Greece to India. Alexander built many cities and introduced Greek **culture** to the people he ruled over.

culture—a people's way of life, ideas, customs, and traditions

THE SEARCH FOR ALEXANDER'S TOMB

When Alexander died, he was buried in Memphis, Egypt. His body was later moved to Alexandria, Egypt. As the city grew, Alexander's tomb was forgotten. There have been hundreds of searches for his tomb. But no one has ever found it.

Alexander led his huge army to defeat the Persian Empire in 330 BC.

ARCHIMEDES

(287-211 BC)

Scientist Archimedes (ar-kuh-MEE-dees) made history one day when he stepped into his bathtub. As he lowered himself into the water, some spilled out. Archimedes discovered that the spilled water equaled the **volume** of his body. Today we call his discovery Archimedes' Principle. Archimedes also invented the **pulley** and a screw pump that lifts water. These inventions are still used today.

volume—the amount of space taken up by an object
pulley—a grooved wheel turned by a rope, belt, or chain that often moves heavy objects

Timeline of Ancient Greece

900 BC

800–700 BC
Homer creates the *Iliad* and the *Odyssey*.

480 BC
Themistocles defeats the Persians at the Battle of Salamis.

432 BC
The building of the Parthenon is completed.

400 BC

387 BC
Plato opens the Academy in Athens.

336 BC
Alexander the Great becomes king of Macedonia at age 20.

146 BC
Greece is made part of the Roman Empire.

100 BC

Glossary

channel (CHA-nuhl)—a narrow stretch of water between two areas of land

city-state (SI-tee-STAYT)—a city that is independent and is not part of a country

culture (KUHL-chuhr)—a people's way of life, ideas, customs, and traditions

democracy (di-MAH-kruh-see)—a kind of government in which the people make decisions by voting

empire (EM-pire)—a large territory ruled by a powerful leader

epic (EP-ik)—relating to a long story, poem, or movie about heroic adventures and great battles

myth (MITH)—a story told by people in ancient times; myths often tried to explain natural events

philosophy (fuh-LOSS-uh-fee)—the study of truth and knowledge

physics (FIZ-iks)—science that studies matter, energy, force, and motion

pulley (PUL-ee)—a grooved wheel turned by a rope, belt, or chain that often moves heavy objects

sculptor (SKUHLP-tur)—a person who creates art by carving stone, wood, or other materials

temple (TEM-puhl)—a building used for worship

volume (VOL-yuhm)—the amount of space taken up by an object

Read More

Bensinger, Henry. *Ancient Greek Government.* Spotlight on Ancient Civilizations: Greece. New York: PowerKids Press, 2014.

Gagne, Tammy. *Homer.* Junior Biography from Ancient Civilizations. Hockessin, Del.: Mitchell Lane Publishers, 2014.

Park, Louise. *Ancient Greece.* Discovery Education: Ancient Civilizations. New York: PowerKids Press, 2013.

Internet Sites

FactHound offers a safe, fun way to find Internet sites related to this book. All of the sites on FactHound have been researched by our staff.

Here's all you do:

Visit *www.facthound.com*

Type in this code: 9781491402757

Super-cool stuff!

Check out projects, games and lots more at
www.capstonekids.com

Critical Thinking Using the Common Core

1. Many things we know today about science and democracy began in ancient Greece. What are some ways ancient Greek leaders and thinkers helped shape our modern world? Use examples from the text to support your answer. (Integration of Knowledge and Ideas)

2. Page 16 describes Plato's ideas for dividing a country's people into three different groups. Do you think his ideas would work in today's world? Explain your answer. (Craft and Structure)

Index